FED
AND
FOCUSED

KAMRYN ADAMS

Published by Impresa Book Group

Impresa Books
New York – Los Angeles – Washington D.C.

10 9 8 7 6 5 4 3 2 1
Copyright © 2017 by Kamryn Adams
All rights reserved

This book or parts thereof may not be reproduced in any form, stored in a retrieval system, or transmitted in any form by any means – electronic, mechanical, photocopy, recording or otherwise – without the prior written permission of the publisher, except as provided by the United States Copyright law

ISBN: 9780990871392 (Paperback)
Library of Congress Control Number: 2017945661

Printed in The United States of America

Unless otherwise indicated, all Scripture quotations are taken from the Holy Bible, New Living Translation, copyright © 1996, 2004, 2007, 2013, 2015 by Tyndale House Foundation. Used by permission of Tyndale House Publishers, Inc., Carol Stream, Illinois 60188. All rights reserved.

GIFTSTEST.COM appears in this publication with the consent of the company abiding by the acceptable use of the terms and conditions. GIFTSTEST.COM is the intellecutal property of The Rock Church San Diego.

For You

May God's glory shine through you wherever you go and whatever you do.

Let your light shine!

Acknowledgements

First, I acknowledge God my creator, who made me specific and unique with a passion to write and to share His love. I am thankful for every step (and misstep) of my journey because without each and every one, I could not have written this book. #teamJESUS

I am ever grateful to my husband and sons for their patience and encouragement during the writing process. Thank you for being the wind beneath my wings. You keep my days purposeful and full of love. #4myboys

To my parents, thank you for continuing to encourage me and, even in adulthood, reminding me to believe I can do anything. #apostlesdaughter #tommysgirl

Thank you to my brothers who shower me with love beyond what any big sister can ask for in life. #bigsistermoments

To my purpose partner, Timothy Davis Jr. You are the engine that drives the Kam machine forward. Your tireless work on my behalf is a blessing and I am continually amazed by your gifts. Your love and friendship push me towards purpose and point me towards heaven. Thank you for listening to me day after day, project after project, event after event, "so forth and so on." #TeamUs

Thank you to my pastor, DeForest Soaries Jr, whose teaching and leadership have focused me on a life of purposeful service in Christ Jesus. I am grateful to my church family at First Baptist Church of Lincoln Gardens; For everyone who has taken the purpose bible study class and helped me to build the curriculum and live it. #FaithinAction

Shout out to my girl, Cheryl Spruill. Surprise!!! I could not have written this book without your love and support as a friend and as a sister in Christ. You kept me sane and reminded me to stay true to my personal beliefs in the storm. Writing this book and teaching Bible study while being chapter President was one of the hardest things I've ever done and you made the difference, girlfriend. You really did. I love you. #presidentsclub

Thank you to everyone who has ever told me to keep going on this purposeful journey. Your words have been a destiny deposit. I love each of you with all of my heart.
#LoveKamryn

Praise for "Stay in Your Lane"

What Readers Are Saying...

"This book gave me a stronger voice to be okay with loving myself and expressing it to people. It is okay to be yourself. You are not defined by your environment."

"After reading this book I feel confident that I am hearing God and moving in the right direction. I feel excited about all the lives that will be impacted as I used my talents within my purpose."

"For the initial page I was hooked. I felt connected one-hundred percent with the author."

"A Staple Life Resource." – AMAZON.com

"FIVE STARS!" – Goodreads.com

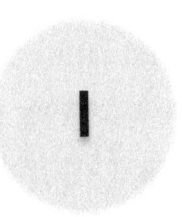

INTRODUCTION

The time has finally come for you to meet Jesus face to face. Your eyes are the size of saucers as you gaze upon his majesty. You have waited your whole life to hear these words. You expect him to say, "Well done, good and faithful servant," but instead he puts a hand on your shoulder and says, "Welcome! How was the meal?"

All these years you've gone to church to be fed. You see the church as a place to serve your spiritual hunger. Guess what? Sitting in the pews and "being fed" week after week is just as unhealthy for your spiritual life as sitting on the sofa and eating cookies and ice cream day after day is for your physical life. You have a greater purpose from God than to sit around and stuff your face with sermons. You've heard a lot of inspirational words during your lifetime. You gobbled them up and were satisfied for a moment. Then, you needed to be fed again. And again. And again. It was never enough to truly satisfy your hunger. You say, "God is good" — which you believe — but your voice fades on "all the time," —because you're not so sure about that.

Maybe you are on the opposite side of this dilemma. You're in five ministries at church, four at-risk youth mentoring programs, three feed the homeless groups, two clean water initiatives, the PTO and you prune the pear tree in the community garden. You are busy. Now, which of those things are you supposed to be doing and which are you doing out of reluctant obligation or the need to feel important?

Here's the good news... finding your purpose will give you the confidence to say, "Yes!" to God and the clarity to say, "No" to people. You'll develop the will and the skill to live your life as God intended you to live: with great passion, peace, and joy. Finding your assignment from God allows you to rest in his sovereignty for provision and protection. When you define 1) who you are, 2) who you are not, and 3) why you're here, you will no longer create your grocery list during the sermon. Instead, you'll be listening for further instruction on your life assignment.

You are on a mission. Your Commanding Officer provides you with daily bread to keep you strong, but eating is not your assignment. You were created with a specific set of talents to do a specific thing at a specific time. God is waiting for you to push away from the table and start working for Him. Everything you do and everywhere you do it should be ON PURPOSE. This is not a church thing. This is a lifestyle. At work, at home, at rest, and on the go — be intentional about what you do and how you do it.

I want you to live the life you were created to live and be happy about it. Don't just get fed. Get focused. Do something! If you picked up this book you must be tired of stuffing your face with religious rhetoric and churchy chatter while the gaping hole on the inside of you keeps you off balance. You keep asking yourself the question "What am I supposed to do?"

Well, you may not have the answers, but God does. You have to ask the one who created you, "Why did you create me?" Go ahead. Take a moment and ask him now.

You'll spend time in prayer, bible study, and hanging out with other people who are walking the journey to purpose. You will start to connect with people who are alive, people who bring you life and you'll let go of relationships that drain your energy and keep you off track.

You are going to spend time thinking about, writing about, praying about, talking about Y-O-U. All your answers will come from the one who created you, not me and not you. I'm only here to point you in the right direction. I'll be the leader but you have to join me on this journey.

Here's how to use this book:

- Pray before you read each chapter. Ask God to speak to you and give you clarity on what he wants you to do and when he wants you to do it.

- Read the reference scriptures. After each chapter read through the scriptures using your Bible or a Bible app on your phone.

-Take the time to think about the Bible Study exercises. Don't rush through them.

-Use the journal pages to write down your thoughts about each chapter and the scripture lessons.

-Talk about it. Talk to people close to you about your experience as your read this book. Ask them for their thoughts on who you are and what you are good at.

-Relax. Don't stress. This is not a timed exercise. Some of you may get it in chapter one and others may go back and read this book three times. Wait on God.

This book is designed to help you grow closer to Christ and commit yourself to the work of God for your life. You will learn about the collective purpose God has for all of us. You'll also discover your individual purpose using the talent and skill he's given you for his glory. You work for God.

Working for God doesn't always mean working as a minister or in the church. We need purposeful people everywhere in every way to shine God's light all over the world. Some of you will read this book and make big changes in what you do. Most of you will read this book and make big changes in how you think about what you do. In each case, your joy and peace will be evident to everyone around you.

Living on purpose allows you to develop a closer relationship with God, our creator. The better you know God, the better you get to know yourself. We study the Bible to learn God's ways so that we can better understand our own. Knowing God, through Jesus, allows you to: know yourself, love yourself, love others, and live on purpose.

As you begin this journey, ask God to help you find the reason he created you. Keep asking him every day. I know you may have heard that you should only pray once and then have faith. But in Luke 18, "The Parable of the Persistent Widow" (v. 1-8), we see that God will answer us when we pray and never give up. Every single time you pick up this book, pray for wisdom and clarity of purpose.

Let's start now....

Dear God, I've taken the first step by reading this book. I want to be everything that you created me to be. I want a life full of your peace and joy. I want to live on purpose. Help me to hear your voice and understand your word. Give me the strength to serve you in all I do. In the name of Jesus Christ our Lord, I pray. Amen.

Journal Your Thoughts

X

PART I

THE PURPOSE

1

IT'S A PROCESS

Think back to when you were eight or nine years old. Who did you want to be when you grew up? If you can't remember what you wanted to be at eight, think about when you were eleven or twelve. Was it a policeman, a teacher, an actor or an astronaut? Is that who you are today? For most of us the answer is a resounding "NO!" What happened along the way that forced you to give up?

Life has a way of twisting and turning our paths before we even know where we're supposed to be going. For most of us, by the time we hit adolescence, messages have come from society, family, friends, and teachers that shape the way we view others and ourselves. We've been told who we are. "You're smart" or "You're lazy." We've also been told who we aren't. "You're not tall enough to play ball" or "Math is not your thing."

These messages shape the path we walk through life. Most of these comments come from people with the best of intentions for us. However, words are a powerful catalyst, often getting us off-track from the life we were created to live. Therefore, many of us don't actually live life. We let life dictate how we live.

As children we wanted laughter and happiness. We wanted fun and adventure. As adults we know we can't have fun all the time but life should not be completely void of the things we enjoy. If you have an emptiness inside of you that keeps crying "there has to be more than this," listen to that voice. That is the voice of God calling you to live on purpose. You have a purpose. Everyone does. In fact, you were a purpose before you were a person. God created you to fill a specific need.

Genesis 2:5-7 says *"For the Lord God had not yet sent rain to water the earth, and <u>there were no people to cultivate the soil</u>. Instead, spring came up from the ground and watered all the land. Then the Lord God formed the man from the dust of the ground. He breathed the breath of life into the man's nostrils, and the man became a living person."* Because the land needed to be cultivated God made Adam. First there was a need and then God created the person to fill that need.

A short time later, God realized something else. Adam needed a helper. Genesis 2:18 says, *"Then the Lord God said, 'It is not good for the man to be alone. <u>I will make a helper who is just right for him.</u>' So the Lord God formed* *from the ground all the wild animals and all the birds of the sky. He brought them to the man to see what he would call them, and the man chose a name for each one. He gave names to all the livestock, all the birds of the sky, and all the wild animals. But still <u>there was no helper just right for him.</u> So the Lord God caused the man to fall into a deep sleep. While the man slept, the Lord God took out one of the man's rib and closed up the opening. Then the Lord God made a woman from the rib, and he brought her to the man."*

Adam needed a helper so God created Eve. She was a purpose before she was a person. In both cases, with Adam and with Eve, there was a need that encouraged the creation of human life. God creates all of us for a specific purpose. The first step in finding your purpose is to accept that you have one. You must realize that there is something that only you can do. I know that's heavy, but it's true. You were created for a specific reason.

Let's get the semantics out of the way. We are going to be talking about "your purpose" but it doesn't belong to you. It is God's purpose for you. If your purpose belonged to you, then you could get out a piece of scratch paper and write down what you want to do with your life. Then it would all come true. But, that's not how it works. You have to consult God, the Creator, on why he created you.

Imagine if your car decided that it wanted to be used for mowing the lawn instead of transporting you from place to place. That's silly! It is equally as silly for you to decide that you want to be someone other than who God created you to be. You car was created to transport you and the lawn mower was created to care for the lawn. If the car starts mowing the grass then what will the lawn mower do? The lawn mower is forced out of its purpose. You see? We all need to be who we were creted to be so that everybody else can be who they were created to be.

Have you ever read the book of Jonah? Oh C'mon! It's only two pages. It begins with, *"The Lord gave this message to Jonah son of Amittai: 'Get up and go to the great city of Nineveh. Announce my judgement against it because I have seen how wicked its people are."* (Jonah 1:1)

Jonah did what so many of us have done when God asks us to be someone we don't want to be or do something we don't want to do. *"But Jonah got up and went in the opposite direction to get away from the Lord."* (Jonah 1:2) Who would do such a thing? All of us. We do it every day of our lives. The good news is that you picked up this book which means you are ready to go to Nineveh, despite the trials you might face.

Spoiler alert! No matter how hard Jonah tried to avoid it, he ended up in Nineveh. He took a long, wet road through the belly of a whale. That was his choice. You have a choice in how you come to your purpose and assignment, but you will ultimately, in some way, do what it is God is asking you to do.

Proverbs 19:21 says, *"Many are the plans of a person's heart, but it the Lord's purpose that prevails."* Don't waste another year trying to be a fish who climbs a tree. Dive in! Be all that God created you to be. Life gets a lot easier when you live on purpose. Purposeful living isn't about having a perfect life. However, the struggles of life are much more tolerable when you know there is a clear reason for each one. Purpose...it's the container that holds peace and passion.

I hate to tell you this, but finding your purpose is only the beginning. It's not even the hardest part. Once you are confident in why you were created, you will then need to live "on purpose." It's exciting. It's fun. But, it's not without trials. One of the reasons we put together the Life Purpose Plan at the end of this book is to help you live out your purpose every day for the rest of your life. When the storms brew around you, you'll need to be reminded of why you were created. Purpose anchors you so that the big bad wolf of life won't huff and puff and blow you down.

In Ephesians 4:1-16, Paul writes to the church of Ephesus about working together. He warns them that they will have conflict and tells them how to handle it. This wonderful group of purposeful, peaceful, passionate people had conflict? Of course, they did. A third of the New Testament is Paul's letters to churches that had drama. Heck! He had to write two letters to the church in Corinth. They were a H-O-T- mess.

Let's take a look at what Paul says. First, he says that we should be humble and loving. Then he says that we should make every effort to keep the peace. He reminds us that we are all here working together with different gifts to accomplish the same goal: to glorify God. Paul makes it sound so easy, right?

It can be a lot easier to work with others if you remember that God is working through you. In 1 Peter 4:11 we are reminded that God's strength is what keeps us living on purpose and in peace. *"If anyone serves, they should do so with the strength God provides so that in all things God may be praised through Jesus Christ. To him be the glory and the power for ever and ever. Amen."* God will give you the strength to do what he created you to do. He will give you the strength to deal with difficult people and circumstances. When you live on purpose, the strength of God carries you along the way.

People! People are a necessary part of this journey and you're going to have to learn how to live with them, work with them and love them every step of the way. They say JOY comes from Jesus, Others, and then Yourself. If you keep these three lined up correctly — Jesus, others and yourself — you will have joy that shines light everywhere you go. God gives us grace and wisdom in dealing with each other so that we can accomplish what he has called us to do.

This process to find your purpose involves prayer, bible study and fellowship with other people. These three things will help you develop a better relationship with God. Once you fall in love with God, you'll be amazed how much more you love yourself. Only then can you truly live out Jesus's words from Mark 12:30-31. *"You must love the Lord your God with all your heart, all your soul and all your mind, and all your strength. The second is equally important: Love your neighbor as yourself. No other commandment is greater than these."*

Jesus commanded us to love others as we love ourselves. That means you must love YOU before you can ever love your neighbor. It takes practice and it's a process. A process we begin today.

So, living for the purpose of God will be like a walk in the rose garden. It has some thorns to avoid, but the sweet fragrance and captivating beauty are worth it. With the help of prayer, scripture and supportive people around you, your life will become a satisfying intersection of joy, peace, passion and productivity.

BIBLE STUDY

Read Proverbs 19:21 a few times aloud. What does this scripture mean to you?

Read Mark 12:30-31. Why do you think Jesus said these were the most important commandments?

Read Luke 18:1-8. Write about a time when someone was so persistent that you gave in to their request because of their determination and passion?

Journal Your Thoughts

2

PRAY

The best place to go for more information on why you were created is The Creator, of course. God created you for a purpose. If you are going to find that purpose you have to spend time with God. Quiet time reflecting on who God is can have great impact on your journey to purpose. The more you understand God who created you; the more you understand yourself. When you know the nature of God, you will better understand how and why He made you. Psalm 139:16 says, *"You saw me before I was born. Every day of my life was recorded in your book. Every moment was laid out before a single day had passed."* God can help you better understand who you are and why you're here.

You're probably wondering how to spend time with someone you've never seen with your eyes. How do you have a conversation with someone who doesn't speak with a mouth? Do you go to him or does he come to you? "Spend time with God" sounds so simple but you don't really know where to begin.

You don't have to get too deep here. There are practical ways for you to spend time with God. Prayer, bible study, and hanging out with other Christians are all ways that we spend time with God. God is everywhere. Psalm 139:7-10 says, *"I can never escape from your Spirit! I can never get away from your presence! If I go up to heaven, you are there. If I go down to the grave you are there. If I ride the wings of the morning, if I dwell by the farthest oceans, even there your hand will guide me and your strength will support me."*

So don't worry. God is with you.

To find your purpose, you're going to have to spend time in prayer. Prayer is simply talking to God. Some people use a majestic voice or flowery poetic words to talk to God. While others speak and have a more formal relationship with God, I just talk to God the same way I talk to you. I may say, "Hey God! I need your help with the quickness." Or "Lord Jesus, please give me enough energy to finish this task." That's prayer – just talking to God.

Jesus tells the disciples in Matthew 6:7-8, *"And when you pray don't babble on and on as the Gentiles do. They think their prayers are answered merely by repeating their words again and again."* If you want to learn more on how to pray, there are thousands of books on how to pray and hundreds of ways to pray. All instruction boils down to what Jesus said in Matthew 6 - Just talk to God.

Jesus gives specific instructions in Matthew 6:5-18. Don't pray for others to hear you like a hypocrite. Go off by yourself and pray to the Father in private. Don't just babble on in prayer trying to impress God. Then, in verse 9 Jesus says, *"Pray like this: Our Father in heaven, may our name be kept holy. May your kingdom come soon. May your will done on the earth, as it is in heaven. Give us today the food we need, and forgive us our sins, as we have forgiven those who sin against us. And don't let us yield to temptation, but rescue us from the evil one."*

The Lord's Prayer. Many of us have memorized it in the King James version from childhood. It's not a poem to be recited but it is a conversation we have with God. When you don't know what to pray, pray the Lord's Prayer. It covers everything you could ask of the Father.

God is not a big, mean bully playing hide and seek with you. He desires to answer your prayers. He wants a relationship with you. God told Jeremiah that he would find Him when he searched with all of his heart. Finding your purpose will take a whole-heart commitment on your part. You'll need to pray and study and talk about it with other Christians. This path to purpose isn't seven steps or ten steps or even twelve steps...it's a journey of many steps over a lifetime.

When you spend time praying to God about your purpose He is guaranteed to answer you. Jeremiah 29:11-13 says, *"For I know the plans I have for you," says the Lord. "They are plans for good and not for disaster, to give you a future and a hope. In those days when you pray, I will listen. If you look for me wholeheartedly, you will find me."*

There are no short cuts on this journey. You'll need to spend time with God beyond Easter, Christmas and Mother's day. God will answer you when you seek him with all of your heart. Using your whole heart means asking him about your purpose more than once. That's why I've asked that you pray before reading every chapter of this book. If you do that you will have prayed at least twelve times about your purpose.

I know. You were taught that you are supposed to pray one time and then have faith. You were taught that praying for something more than once is disrespectful to the all-knowing God. Well, I'm here to tell you — wait for it — you were taught wrong.

In Luke 18 Jesus teaches the disciples about an unjust Judge who was annoyed by a persistent widow. *"The judge ignored her for a while, but finally he said to himself, 'I don't fear God or care about people, but this woman is driving me crazy. I'm going to see that she gets justice, because she is wearing me out with her constant requests!'"* (Luke 18:4-5)

Jesus told them, *"Learn a lesson from this unjust judge. Even he rendered a just decision in the end. So don't you think God will surely give justice to his chosen people who cry out to him day and night? Will he keep putting them off? I tell you, he will grant justice to them quickly!"* (v. 6-8) This passage of scripture lets us know that persistence in prayer and seeking wisdom from God is more than just a one time action. It's a habit.

This persistence in prayer is not for God, but for us. Have you ever been to the store with a small child? They find something in every aisle that they want. "Mommy can I have..." something that they have seen. "Daddy can we get..." the new thing they saw on TV. Good parents do not flex to every whim of their children. They understand that the child is reacting to the current stimulation of what they have seen. God is a good parent. He knows what we should have and should not.

In the parable of the persistent widow, she wanted justice – a very reasonable request. The judge – uncaring as he was – was moved not just because she kept knocking but because her passion for what she wanted finally moved him to action. God wants you to know your purpose and he will answer you. Keep asking.

You want to know the most important aspect of prayer? It's not a deep theological understanding. It's not the way you enunciate or the number of different names you can call God. The most important aspect of prayer is to expect an answer. *"Keep on asking and you will receive what you ask for. Keep on seeking and you will find. Keep on knocking, and the door will be opened to you. For everyone who asks, receives. Everyone who seeks, finds. And to everyone who knocks the door will be opened."* (Matthew 7:7-8)

God looks at our hearts in everything we do. When you pray believe in your heart that you will get an answer from God. Expect it. Look for answers all around you. You'll find them when you seek them with all of your heart.

Isn't that why you are reading this book? You are looking for answers to your purpose.

Listen and you'll receive them. Pray before reading each chapter. Pray before reading your Bible. Pray. Just talk to God.

BIBLE STUDY

Read Matthew 6:6-13. What can you remove from your daily life and add quality time with God?

Read Psalm 139:7-10 aloud a few times. How would you behave differently if you realized God was always with you?

What is it that you are waiting on God to do in your life? Have you been persistent in your prayer about this thing?

There are 10,080 minutes in a week. Write out a schedule for spending time with God during the week. What percentage of time is it?

Example: Monday 7:30 am Prayer (10 minutes)

MONDAY: _____

TUESDAY: _____

WEDNESDAY: _____

THURSDAY: _____

FRIDAY: _____

SATURDAY: _____

SUNDAY: _____

WEEKLY TIME WITH GOD: _____
% of MY WEEK :
(Number of minutes/10,080 x 100)

Journal Your Thoughts

3

GET PREPARED

We established in the previous chapter that prayer is an important step in this journey to finding your purpose. Equally important is reading and studying the Bible. Prayer is talking to God. Bible study is listening to God. This is why we pray before we read our Bibles. We want to hear God's response through his word. Studying God's word helps prepare you to live on purpose.

Bible study is so much easier than it used to be. When I was a young girl, I read my Bible every night before I went to bed. I struggled night after night through the "thee" and "thou" of the King James version. In high school I discovered the New International Version. Boy! I was glad. It changed my entire Bible study experience. Now, there are Bible apps for your phone, websites and newsletters that can deliver the Bible passages to you every day. There are many different translations of the Bible for you to read. Find the one that suits your personality and learning style best.

There are three main kinds of translations defined by how it interprets the original Hebrew (Old Testament) and Greek (New Testament) manuscripts. You can get word-for-word translations, thought-for-thought translations and paraphrased translations. This book uses the New Living

Translation, a blend of thought-for-thought and paraphrase technique. It essentially takes the original Hebrew and Greek and aligns it with contemporary English language. My favorite word-for-word translation is the New King James version. It's basically the KJV without "thee" and "thou" and words ending in "-th." The New International Version (NIV) is my thought-for-thought choice. The Message Bible is a paraphrased version of the Bible. Many people like that one, too.

Like all assignments, you'll need to be prepared for this purpose journey. Discovering your purpose and having the courage to live intentionally for God will take preparation on your part. Preparing for purpose begins with knowing God. We get to know God through reading and studying the Bible. When you understand who God is you will understand what He has created you to do.

Equally important is knowing the things that God definitely would not tell you to do.

"My sheep listen to my voice; I know them, and they follow me." (John 10:27) It's frustrating to hear people say God told them to harm someone, to steal or lie. Those things aren't in the nature of God. Reading the Bible helps you understand and get clear on who God is and who He is not. Your purpose is not to sell drugs, to defraud people or glorify sin in the world. That is not something God would have you to do. All of these things are talked about in the Bible.

God has used your entire life to prepare you for this moment. Think of all the things that have led to you reading this book. The mistakes you've made, the people who have come and gone in your life, the burning desire for more...none of it was a mistake. It was all to land you right where you sit at this moment reading this book. Maybe you found this book on an airplane. Isn't that cool? You were meant to read this book right now. You may have bought the book months ago, even years ago but now you decided to take it out and read it. You're not too late. You're right on time. Remember, Psalm 139 tells us that all the pages of our life were written before the first day of life began. On this page of your life story, you've decided to find your purpose.

Timing is everything

Esther was a young woman filled with purpose. On the exterior, she was a beautiful woman who had become King Xerxes favorite lady because of her looks. Underneath that beauty and grace, there was boldness and wisdom. Esther was my kind of woman. She knew how to pray and slay.

I encourage you to read the Book the Esther on your own, but I'll give you some background. King Xerxes and his boys were having a party and it got a little out of hand. They were drunk. The king was so drunk that he called for his wife, Vashti, to dance and show off her beauty for his friends. She refused to come dance in a room of drunken men. Though Vashti gets quite a bit of flack from pulpits on Sunday morning, (sans theology) I appreciate her for refusing to be used as a symbol of pride and lust. But...that's another book.

Vashti's defiance made the other men nervous so they encouraged Xerxes to banish her. *"Queen Vashti has wronged not only the king but also every noble and citizen throughout your empire. Women everywhere will begin to despise their husbands when they learn that Queen Vashti has refused to appear before the king."* (Esther 1:16-17) Xerxes was influenced by his friends so he sent his wife away. Note: Don't let the voices of others determine how you will function in your relationship...also another book.

Once Xerxes was no longer angry and embarrassed he began to miss Vashti and regret that he had banished her. So, his personal attendants decided that he should search for a new queen. Many beautiful young women were brought into the royal harem. One of these women was Esther, a young Jewish woman being raised by her Uncle, Mordecai.

Mordecai instructed Esther to keep her identity silent. She was not to tell anyone that she was a Jew. As time when on, she became Xerxes favorite and he appointed her Queen. At the same time there was a man in the kingdom named Haman, whom the king had recently promoted. His promotion called for all the king's men to bow to him. Mordecai, being faithful to Jewish custom, refused to bow. This enraged Haman and he convinced King Xerxes that the Jewish people and their Jewish customs were a threat to the current way of life. Again, Xerxes was so easily influenced by his boys. He scheduled the complete annihilation of the Jews on March 7th of the following year.

This is made for TV drama. His queen, Esther, was a Jew, but he had no idea. When

Mordecai heard of the decree he went to Esther and told her that she must go before King Xerxes to stop him. Esther said, "Say what?" Actually she said, *"All the king's officials and even the people in the provinces know that anyone who appears before the king in his inner court without being invited is doomed to die unless the king holds out his gold scepter. The king has not called for me to come to him for thirty days."* Esther 4:11-13

Mordecai responded to Esther to help her put things in perspective. He said to her, *"Don't think for a moment that because you're in the palace you will escape when all the other Jews are killed"* ...girlfriend. (Esther 4:13) Okay, I added that last part.

He went on to explain to Esther that this was her destiny moment. Everything in her life up to that point prepared her to be a great help for the Jewish people. God made her Xerxes' favorite lady. He had made her smart and beautiful and devoted to God. He made her bold. God made her all that she was for that moment in time.

Esther decided it was time to prepare. She went on a three day fast and prayed to the Lord for guidance. Once she got her assignment, she was resolute. This is why I love her so much. After praying and fasting, she would go before the king. She knew the danger it represented and I'm sure she was afraid. But, when God calls you to purpose, you can't help but respond to the call. Esther realized that this was the reason she was born. This moment; This task; This great opportunity to do good in the world. Esther moves forward and says, *"If I must die, I must die." (*Esther 4:16)

Once you learn your purpose, you are willing to risk everything to do what God created you to do. There is a defining moment in everyone's life. It may not be as dramatic as saving an entire population of people, but your moment will come. Make a decision to "do good" for God rather than pursue selfish comfort.

Right now you're thinking, "What if I missed it?" Impossible! The burning desire you have to find your purpose at this time in your life is the beginning of your preparation. You haven't missed it. Your defining moment is coming and, like Esther, you will be prepared.

Reading the Bible will prepare you to do what God has created you to do. This is your time. You are reading this book exactly when it is time for you to read it. Psalm 139 tells us that your story was written before you were born. Genesis 2 illustrates that you were a purpose before you were a person.

It's your choice. You can live the grand biography God has written for you or you can ignore that burning desire for "more" and just let life toss you around aimlessly until you die. Choose God like Mary did in Luke 1:38. *"Mary responded, 'I am the Lord's servant. May everything you have said about me come true."*

BIBLE STUDY

Read the Book of Esther. What lessons do you learn about God's purpose and timing?

Write about a time in your life when God was working in the background to help you with a situation that you didn't realize until later.

Journal Your Thoughts

4

Get Confirmed

There will be people who are an important part of your journey. They are your "purpose partners." It is impossible to live an intentional life alone. You need purpose partners walking with you. Your purpose partners are not clones. They should not think like you, talk like you, and like the same things you like. They should be people who share your love of God and belief in purposeful living.

They should inspire you, not hinder you. They should encourage you, not disparage you. Most importantly they should help grow the spiritual fruit in your life, not squeeze the life from it.

Purpose partners are here to confirm what God has said. Repeat after me...CONFIRM! If you have always loved art and believe God has called you to be a painter, he's not going to send someone to tell you that you are supposed to study aeronautical engineering and work at NASA. Whatever someone tells you "from God" will already be planted in your heart and it will resonate with you in some way. This is why it is critically important for you to spend time with God in prayer and bible study.

How well do you know yourself? You need to develop confidence in the abilities that God has given you. Know what you do well. You also need to know your passion. Know what you love to do. This will help you better understand your purpose.

When you spend time with God, you get to know yourself better. If you don't understand who you are, all the advice you get will have you jumping hurdles and running zig zags, which makes this journey longer and more difficult than it needs to be. People can only confirm what the Lord has told you to do. Say it one more time aloud, "Confirm!"

There are two parts to this purpose equation. First, you must have a passion to do what it is you are called to do. God will plant the passion for his purpose inside of you. *"Take delight in the Lord, and he will give you your heart's desires."* (Psalm 37:4) Second, you must be good at it. Just because you like to do something, doesn't necessarily mean you have the skill to do it. *"God has given each of you a gift from his great variety of spiritual gifts. Use them well to serve one another."* (1 Peter 4:10) We'll talk more in detail about these two aspects later. However, it's important you keep these in mind when people come to confirm what God has purposed you to do.

God looks on the heart and if you keep your heart aligned with Him, he will make sure you get to your purpose and he'll use your purpose partners to confirm the way. Psalm 37:4 is so often used out of context. When you read it in the contemporary English context it reads as if God will give us whatever we want. It suggests that we can just "blab it and grab it." However, the word "delight" here comes from the Hebrew word "anog" which means to be soft or pliable like a primitive root. Therefore, if you are rooted in Christ and make yourself flexible to the ways of God, the things you desire will be from God. God will give you the desire of your heart — meaning he will plant a desire in you for what you were created to do.

A great illustration of this concept occurs in the ninth chapter of the book of Acts. Saul was on his way to Damascus to capture Christians and bring them back to Jerusalem.

He believed that Christians were blasphemous. He was passionate and sincere about stopping these people from dishonoring God. Note: You can be sincere in your efforts for God, but be sincerely wrong about it.

Acts 9 tells us about Saul's conversion to becoming Paul, an apostle of Jesus Christ. *"As he was approaching Damascus on this mission, a light from heaven suddenly shone down around him."* (Acts 9:3) When you are on the wrong path, but your heart believes you are doing the right thing for God, a light will shine and show you the correct way to do things. God looked upon Saul's heart, not his mistaken actions.

Jesus tells Saul that he is incorrect in his thinking and then gives him further instruction. *"I am Jesus, the one you are persecuting! Now get up and go into the city, and you will be told what you must do."* (Acts 9:5-6) The light from Jesus blinded Saul and he was unable to see for three days. You may have already figured out that things need to change in your life. However, it may take some time to figure out exactly what you should be doing. Saul had to wait for further instruction and so might you.

In verse 10, Jesus sends Ananias to go to Saul. *"Go over to Straight Street to the house of Judas. When you get there, ask for a man from Tarsus named Saul. He is praying to me right now. I have shown him a vision of a man named Ananias coming in and laying hands on him so he can see again."* The Lord lined it all up with Saul and Ananias. He sent Ananias and he told Saul Ananias was coming.

So, when Ananias did what the Lord told him to do — lay hands on Saul to restore his vision — there was no confusion or conflict. They didn't argue about whether or not the Lord really sent him because the Lord had already told Saul that Ananias was coming. Ananias didn't come lay hands on Saul's ears so he could hear. He did exactly as the Lord told him. No more. No less. He restored Saul's sight. When you and your purpose partners are aligned with God, God will eliminate any confusion and senseless conflict. Ananias CONFIRMED what the Lord had shown Saul.

You see, God is not trying to trick you. He wants you to discover your purpose. He wants you to have clarity and wisdom in how to live. Make your life flexible to God's ways and he will ensure that you are on the right path. God is the authority on your purpose. It is His purpose for you. Because Saul was sincere in his desire to serve the Lord, Jesus came and corrected his thinking. He went on to become a great apostle who established many churches and wrote a third of the New Testament scriptures.

If God can correct a guy who set out to kill and imprison Christians, I'm pretty sure he can get you from the choir stand to the deacon board. I am absolutely positive that he can get you into the right job to match your skills and passion. I guarantee you that God will set your life on a purpose path that brings you joy, peace, passion and love. The Bible says, *"Trust in the Lord with all your heart; do not depend on your own understanding. Seek his will in all you do, and he will show you which path to take."* (Proverbs 3:5)

BIBLE STUDY

What three (3) people in your life can serve as purpose partners?

Read Psalm 37:4 a few times aloud. What does that scripture mean to you? What areas do you need to allow God to plant desires in your heart?

Read about Saul's conversion in Acts 9, write about a time in your life when God shined a light and helped you correct your thinking about something? What did you do differently afterwards?

Journal Your Thoughts

Get Together

If you want to know why you were created, spend time with the creator. The more you get to know God, the better you will know yourself. I'll continue to say that over and over until it is planted in your heart and mind. You must spend time with God to find your purpose. There is no other way.

Have you ever had deep regard for a person because of their character or skill? We do it with sports figures and entertainers all the time. We watch them do what they do and begin to elevate them to a higher status. There is no one higher than God. He is the reason Beyonce can dance and Lebron can dunk. He's the reason Tom Brady has a Superbowl ring on every finger and Drake has more Grammys than his two hands can hold. Just as we admire the attributes of the people God created, we must remember to worship The Creator of those attributes.

The primary reason you were created is to worship God. I repeat. Your first purpose in life is to worship God. It's not to be a teacher or a movie star. It's not to be a fire fighter or a ballerina. You were created, first and foremost, to worship God. Worship deepens our relationship with Christ by providing us with an intimate experience to know Him better.

We have a collective purpose as humans that requires us to be together in worship and fellowship. We gather together to encourage one another to live a common faith. The book of Acts is a record of the early church. We learn how the early Christians came together to form a community. Living a purposeful life requires community. You cannot do it alone.

"All the believers devoted themselves to the apostles' teaching, and to fellowship, and to sharing in meals, (including the Lord's supper), and to prayer." Acts 2:42 gives us a model for being together as Christians. We should commit ourselves to study, fellowship and prayer. The early church also pulled their resources to give to the poor. Acts 2:45 tells us *"They sold their property and possessions and shared the money with those in need."*

You can see that the early church was established ON PURPOSE. They did all the things that they were created to do: worship God, fellowship with people, give of time, talent and resources, talk about Jesus, and serve others.

Did you catch that? You were created to do five things. So if you picked up this book to find a quick reference guide to purpose, there it is. You're finished. Our collective purpose, above all else, is to do those things. How we do those things in our individual lives is our specific assignment from God.

We get together with other like-minded Christians so that we can access the power of fellowship. Being around other Christians allows us to build relationships that are beneficial to us naturally and spiritually. We begin to do business with other purposeful people. We socialize with other purposeful people. We travel with purposeful people. Intentional living is a lifestyle and so when you get together with other people who believe what you believe, you tap into powerful living.

Being together also allows you to help more people. You can pull your resources and have a bigger impact in service to others. You were not created to sit at home alone. You were meant to be with other people. Even if your personality type is less than social. You can fellowship with a small group of friends or join a more task-focused ministry at church. No matter how God developed your personality, He never intended for you to go through life alone.

Another benefit to hooking up with other people is that it helps you grow in faith. Spending time alone with God is critical to building an intimate relationship with Him. But you must also spend time with others in worship and Bible study to grow. Fellowship is an exchange that is beneficial to all parties. Not only will you grow in understanding but you will also help others grow by sharing your learning and experience. Hanging out with other Christians helps you grow in your faith.

Hebrews 10:24-25 teaches us, *"Lets us think of ways to motivate one another to acts of love and good works. And let us not neglect our meeting together as some people do, but encourage one another, especially now that the day of his return is drawing near."* Living for Christ in contemporary society is not easy. There are plenty of distractions and misrepresentations of "good" that can pull you away from your faith. This departure from faith is also a departure from purpose. In order to live ON PURPOSE you must stay connected to other people who share the faith.

So where is the best place for you hang out with other Christians? Church. Don't give me the side eye. No, you do not have to attend church to get to Heaven. However, fellowshipping with other Christians and participating in corporate worship can greatly enhance your life here on earth.

We are saved by God's grace. The only thing you must do to get to Heaven is believe. *"If you openly declare that Jesus is Lord and believe in your heart that God raised him from the dead, you will be saved."* (Romans 10:9) However, holding on to that belief in an age of skepticism when popular culture pulls us from biblical wisdom can be tough without the help of other Christians.

Let's establish this up front. You are the church. Many people neglect attending worship services at "church" because they embrace the notion that they are the church. Yes, you are the church. However, you are also called to fellowship with other believers to accomplish the purpose God has for His church.

"But what is fellowship? Who says I have to go to church to be in fellowship?" I hear you. So let's handle this quickly and move on.

You do not have to go to church to be in fellowship. However, for the purposes of Christianity, fellowship is coming together like the early church in Acts. Going out for drinks with your friends and watching a boxing match is not fellowship UNLESS you talked about Jesus, studied your Bible, gave to the poor or served others...and not just beer across the table.

In Matthew 18:20 (NIV) Jesus said, *"Where two or three gather together in my name, there I am with them."* It's not just about gathering together. It's gathering together IN HIS NAME. Otherwise, meeting up at the strip club would be church...and to be clear...it is not.

So, the best place to gather with a group of believers is at that building with the stained glass windows, pews/seats and a lectern. For simplicity sake we'll call it church. When you attend a bible-focused church, it is impossible not to learn more about what you believe. Hearing the preacher on Sunday mornings, helps you learn about the faith. *"So faith comes from hearing, that is, hearing the Good News about Christ."* (Romans 10:17)

Attending church service helps strengthen your commitment to the faith. It reminds you that you are not alone in this journey to purpose. There are other people who look like you and live where you live that desire "more" from life. You can find them at church.

Let me guess. You were very involved in church once and it was a disaster. So, you decided to worship in your home listening to various television ministries. Your relationship with God is personal and one-on-one. That's cool. Being alone may work for worship but it does not work for the purpose of fellowship.

Remember the woman at the well in the Book of John? You know, the one who had five husbands and was living with her boyfriend. She got into a debate with Jesus about where to worship. Her people believed that worship was to occur on Mount Gerizim, where her ancestors worshipped. She knew that the Jews — and Jesus was Jewish — insisted that worship must take place in Jerusalem.

Imagine her surprise when Jesus said, *"Believe me dear woman, the time is coming when it will no longer matter whether you worship the Father on this mountain or in Jerusalem."* (John 4:21) Worship is an experience that can take place anywhere, alone or with others. It is an intimate encounter with God. There is only one requirement for worship. In John 4:23-24 Jesus gives us specific instructions for worship. *"But the time is coming — indeed it's here now — when true worshipers will worship the Father in spirit and in truth. The Father is looking for those who will worship him that way. For God is Spirit, so those who worship him must worship in spirit and in truth."*

No, it's not required of you to be in church on Sunday morning to worship. But finding a church home for regular worship will greatly enhance your life and your efforts to live on purpose. Worship and fellowship with others can help you develop a greater sense of purpose and guide you on the journey to intentional living. You can't do this alone.

I know that finding a church is not an easy task, especially since we have our preferences for what we want in a church: good preaching, good music, plenty of parking and climate control. Instead of looking at church as a place to serve others, we often look for our churches to keep us fed. We want to be fed without helping to stock the refrigerator.

We choose our church based on preaching style or the kind of music we want to hear. Sometimes, we may find a church we absolutely love but it's just too far to go on Sunday morning, let alone mid-week bible study class. If the service goes too long, we complain. If we don't have good parking or comfortable seats, we complain. This is not the attitude we should have towards our fellowship with other Christians.

When you go to church, you should go with a mind to worship God and to help others worship him. You go to church to celebrate who God is and encourage others to do the same. You celebrate with those who are celebrating and you offer compassion to those who are in pain. *"Be happy with those who are happy and weep with those who weep."* (Romans 12:15)

When you pray at church, pray for others in the sanctuary to know Jesus. You can pray for your own stuff at home. Try going into the church and praying for those around you. Pray for the family with the small children beside you. Pray for the man who appears to be alone in the back of the church. And please….pray for the preacher that is bringing the word of God to the congregation. When you go to church, don't always go to be fed. Go to serve — God and others.

BIBLE STUDY

Read Acts 2:14-47. How did Peter's obedience to God's call on his life impact who we are today as a church? How can you impact those around you to live more purposeful lives for God?

Read Matthew 18:20 three times aloud. How can you spend more time socializing with Christians? What activities can you do to incorporate God's presence into your time with others?

Examine your attitude about church. Why did you choose your church home?

Journal Your Thoughts

Do Something

A disciple of Christ — a person who follows Jesus, a Christian — has a specific assignment to use his or her skills and talents for the purpose of helping others. You have to do something. Your specific assignment is not to become rich, though walking in your purpose may make you rich. It is not for you to become famous, though when you start living on purpose you may become famous. The reason God created you is to be of service to others in a specific way unique to your skills, abilities and passion.

Paul explains it to us in Ephesians 2:10. *"For we are God's masterpiece. He has created us anew in Christ Jesus, so we can do the good things he planned for us long ago."* You were created to do good, not harm. God planned for you to live on purpose long ago. Your purpose is to do the good things he has planned.

Doing for God can become a distraction that pulls you away from God, if you aren't careful. Don't get so caught up in "doing" for God that you are no longer being for God. We are human BEings, not human DOings. You can shine the light of God through who you are, not just by what you do.

Doing for God can also become an obsession. Service to others is a part of your purpose but you cannot work your way into being a good person. Perhaps that's why before we get to Ephesians 2:10 Paul makes it clear in verses 8 and 9 that we are saved by God's grace not our own good works. *"God saved you by his grace when you believed. And you can't take credit for this; it is a gift from God. Salvation is not a reward for the good things we have done, so none of us can boast about it."*

When God saved us by his grace, he assigned us to serve other people. However, you cannot neglect God in your service efforts to others. Regardless of how many ministries and non-profit boards you sit on, if you are not worshipping God, you are not living on purpose. You can't be the head usher *every* Sunday. You can't be in the parking lot directing traffic during *every* service. If you serve every Sunday, then find another time when you will worship the Lord and work on your relationship with him.

You have to take the time to be with God in order to work for God. On our jobs we have staff meetings and 1-on-1 meetings to align and clarify goals and objectives. Your time with God in prayer, worship and bible study is a staff meeting to help clarify the assignment and purpose he has for you.

When we serve, we want to serve with the attitude of Christ. Philippians 2 gives us a model. It tells us to *"... agree wholeheartedly with each other, loving one another, and working together with one mind and purpose."* (v. 2) Then the scripture goes on to say, *"Don't be selfish. Don't try to impress others. Be humble, thinking of others as better than yourselves." (v. 3)* For real?! Paul makes it sound so easy.

Everybody has his or her own motivation for serving. How can we work together with one mind and one purpose if we all have different reasons for serving? Well, the overarching purpose for which we all serve is for God's glory — to shine His light into the darkness of another person's life. Your purpose is to be WHO YOU ARE and let other people know that God is good and He loves them.

As people watch God shine through your life they will come to believe and serve him, too. In Mathew 14, Peter asked to walk on water. Jesus granted his request. *"But when he saw the strong wind and the waves, he was terrified and began to sink."* (v.30) Jesus grabbed Peter and put him back in the boat. The Bible tells us that when they got back in the boat the wind stopped. *"Then the disciples worshiped him. 'You really are the son of God!' they exclaimed."* (v.33) When you live to honor God, even when you sink from fear, the Lord shines light around you and others will see and believe.

When we feed a homeless person or smile at a lonely child on the bus, we are shining a piece of light into darkness. When we read a story to a classroom of children or host an exercise class for adults, we care for others and encourage them. If it's good, it's God.

We've established that whenever we serve for good, we serve for God. As long as we are in service to others, God is happy, right? So let's get these volunteer hours over with and get on with our day. Just hold your nose and clean up the trash on the side of the road. Just ignore that sister or mister that works your last nerve and keep serving. We just need to get it done for God. Right?

Wrong! Read down to Philippians 2:14-15. You ready? Take a deep breath. This is it.... *"Do everything without complaining and arguing, so that no one can criticize you. Live clean, innocent lives as children of God, shining like bright lights in a world full of crooked and perverse people."* Wait! Everything? Yes, everything. When we serve we should not do it begrudgingly or out of dispassionate obligation. We are to serve with joy in our hearts for the work and for the people.

One of the ways you know you are serving in your purpose is that you serve with the grace of God. This means that you are the right person for the job. Not that purposeful living is perfect and without trials. You will have conflicts. However, because you are driven by purpose, God sustains you. These conflicts will be easier for you to handle than someone else who has not been called for the task.

Have you ever had someone say, "I don't know how you do it?" Not everyone has the ability to do what you do. There are areas of serving that just come naturally to you. While some people hate to entertain and find it a burden, you are delighted and full of energy when you can host people and show them love. While some people hate making decisions and being responsible for others, you love to set the vision and direction for what needs to be done. These are examples of working in your purpose with the grace of God. He gives you the ability to get the job done, even through the tough times. And there will be tough times...

In Matthew 20:20-28 Jesus teaches us more about serving. This passage of scripture reveals quite a bit about group dynamics when serving with others. Remember, everybody is coming to serve with their own agenda and you'll have to figure out how to serve without complaining.

The mother of James and John came to Jesus and asked that her sons be seated next to him in heaven. Can you imagine? As parents we all love our children, but I hope nobody reading this book thinks that their child is equal to Jesus. The request was absurd. Jesus answered her by saying, *"You don't know what you are asking! Are you able to drink from the bitter cup of suffering I am about to drink?"* (Matthew 20:22)

As humans we tend to be dissatisfied with what God has given us and we envy the lives of others. You know how it goes. Singers want to act and actors want to rap. Athletes want to sing and rappers want to play basketball. Everybody is searching for that thing — the thing called "more." Here's why… if you only sing for money and fame, there is a gaping hole inside of you that acting won't fill. If you only act for the applause, you'll have a thirst for acceptance that never gets quenched. You must do something in service of others. This is why you see Hollywood humanitarians like Angelina, Will and Jada. There has to be "more" than money and attention.

It can be very dangerous to desire the gifts and talents of others. We often want a different life than the one that we've been given by God. This is a hidden source of frustration. We're frustrated because we do not yet understand the purpose for our own lives. We look at the next person and think they have it so much better than we do.

We often look at the end result of another person's journey and wish to trade places. We want the glory without knowing the story. We envy the success without knowing the sacrifice. Was James' and John's mother asking that they be crucified with Jesus? Of course not. She had no idea of the sacrifice that would take place to become King of kings and Lord of lords. She simply wanted her sons to be like Jesus.

So many times we look at other people and want our lives to be the same, without truly understanding the sacrificial path of purpose they've walked. When we force our lives to be more or less than God's grande biography for us, we open ourselves to depression, anxiety, sorrow and deep frustration. Most times we don't even understand why we feel like we do. We know something is missing and the only thing we can call it is "more."

Now, when the other disciples heard that James and John were trying to get a hook up, they got angry. I'm sure each of them felt that they had the right to sit next to Jesus in

Heaven, as well. At that point, Jesus called them all together. Why? Because when serving with others, it's best to address conflict early and often. Those who are called to leadership know that ignoring a small ripple of discontent in a working group can lead to a huge wave of destruction later. Learn a lesson from Jesus. When you are working with others, address small issues before they become big ones. Do it now. Stop reading. Pick up the phone and handle it.

Jesus explained to them the true meaning of service. This is a truth that still stands firm today in our families, churches and civic organizations. He said that people flaunt their authority and throw their weight around to seem important. *"But among you it will be different. Whoever wants to be a leader among you must be your servant, and whoever wants to be first among you must become your slave." (Matthew 20:27)* Jesus teaches us that true leadership is service to those whom you lead. It means — as I like to say — taking one for the team.

Jesus tells us that even he, the Messiah, came to serve. *"For even the Son of man came not to be served but to serve others and to give his life as a ransom for many."* If you want to be satisfied with your life, be prepared to serve others. It's the only path to purpose.

This path is not a journey of contemplation or feelings. It's an assignment to "DO" something. Purpose is more than just the feeling of contentment that you are in the right space in your life. Sure, living on purpose feels good. But purposeful living means you must actually do something with the skills and talent you have to make a difference in the lives of others.

Can you get anything out of serving others? Of course. Can you use your talent to make money? Of course, you can. You can even be motivated by notoriety or acclaim. However, money and fame cannot be your primary motivation for service. The reason we use our skills in service is to shine God's light into the dark places of life. We serve to let others know we love them. More importantly, we want them to know that God loves them. Your purpose is to serve others with everything you have.

BIBLE STUDY

Read and reflect on Philippians 2:1-18. Examine your attitude towards serving others. Write down the areas where you are similar to the scripture. Now, write the areas where you need to improve. Be specific.

What is your motivation for serving? Are there areas in your life where you grumble and complain about your duty to serve? i.e. marriage, parenthood, caring for an elderly parent, etc.

Read Matthew 20:20-28. Think about a time when you wanted your life to be like someone else's. What did you learn from that? What aspects of your life might other's envy? What sacrifice or cost might they be ignoring?

When Jesus said, "You will indeed drink from my bitter cup," what do you think he meant? Reflect on a time when you got what you asked for and later regretted it. What did you learn from that experience?

Journal Your Thoughts

7

Give something

So far we've covered three things that everybody was created to do: 1) worship God, 2) fellowship with people 3) serve others. The next purpose we all have is to give. God provides for us so that we can provide for others as a form of service. Yes, giving includes time and talent but it also includes giving of your resources: money and things that cost money.

The first thing you need to know about purposeful giving is that it must come from a sincere desire in your heart. 2 Corinthians 9:7 tells us that, *"You must each decide in your heart how much to give. And don't give reluctantly or in response to pressure for God loves a person who gives cheerfully."* So, don't give because you feel pressured after reading this chapter. Hopefully, by the time you finish this chapter you will understand why God wants us to give and why it is part of our purpose to give to others.

Giving is defined as "to put into the possession of another for his or her use." That means that when we truly give by definition there are no strings attached. When it comes to giving, we often do so with a consumer's attitude. What do I get if I give? What power or notoriety can I get from giving? How much control will I have over what I give?

We do have expectations for our giving and rightfully so. If you give on purpose then you should expect that your giving produces some kind of good work. *"And God is able to bless you abundantly, so that in all things at all times, having all that you need, you will abound in every good work."* (1 Corinthians 9:8) Your resources — money, time and talent — are all for the purpose of good work. So yes, there is an expectation with your giving that it produces something good.

When we give to our churches we expect them to do something good with it. We expect them to be responsible and to use the money for the purposes of spreading the gospel and caring for others. However, that expectation should not become an obstacle to our giving. We must change our minds about how we give to the church and realize that we are not giving to the pastor — no matter what kind of car he drives. We are not giving to a building — no matter how grande it may be. When we put money into that offering plate, we are giving back to God. We are fulfilling our purpose to give. The church leadership is responsible for any use or misuse. Reflect on the dictionary definition — to put in the possession of another for his or her own use. Once you drop the money into the plate, it's no longer your concern.

Although we give without condition, we must still use wisdom in giving. If you learn — not simply hear it through gossip — but if you learn by evidence that a beneficiary of your gift is not using the resource for good works, then you need to shift your giving. Be prayerful. If the resources are being used for destructive, selfish, or ungodly reasons, then — and only then — do you find another beneficiary for your resources. You do not stop giving. But, you shift to a more purposeful cause. For example, you would not continue to give your nephew money for rent when you find out he uses it to gamble. However, if you find out he sometimes uses it to put gas in his car or to buy a book, you should not be upset.

Most of us are not greedy misers who refuse to give. Our attitude toward giving is that we give when we have enough to give. But when is that? If you won't give me ten dollars from a hundred you certainly won't give a hundred thousand from a million dollars. We lie to ourselves thinking that if we have more we will start to give more.

This mindset will change as we pursue purposeful living. Giving on purpose is to give from what we have, not from what we have left. Instead of only giving our old clothes and buying ourselves new ones, we might buy new clothes to give to a homeless shelter and keep our old clothes if we can still fit them. Rather than donating our old furniture to the community center, maybe we could buy new furniture for the community center and keep our old sofa a little while longer.

Giving is a mindset that takes practice. We want to have our IRAs maxed out and our savings accounts full before we start to give.

That is not purposeful giving. Anybody without a heart of coal would do that. But those who desire to live on purpose and find satisfaction in life are people who give cheerfully and generously.

One of the reasons we are not as generous as we need to be is fear. You are afraid you might not have enough when you need it. We save up for a rainy day — just in case. Jesus addresses this mentality in Matthew 6:19. He says, *"Don't store up treasures here on earth, where moths eat them and rust destroys them, and where thieves break in and steal."* In verse 21 Jesus says, *"Wherever your treasure is, there the desires of your heart will also be."*

The more "stuff" we have the more our identity is tied to having stuff. We tend to lose our sense of being and focus only on the material things we can possess, all of which can be stolen or destroyed in a moment. Jesus warns that we cannot "serve God and be enslaved to money." (v.24)

Of course, no Christian believes that they would put money before God. No way! We would never serve money over God. Well, let's examine it. Let's say you are a highly paid executive at a Fortune 50 company right now. After reading this book you feel a tug on your heart to leave your job and go work with at-risk youth. You have worked with youth programs in the past and you genuinely believe in the cause. However, you have a huge house and nice cars. You have daughters that take dance classes and sons that attend exclusive sports camps. You just can't do it. You can't afford to do what God is leading you to do. In this situation, who is the master? God or money?

Or maybe you own a business and a colleague has shown you some "special" accounting techniques that can save you on taxes by not reporting all of your income. You need the increased cash flow in your business.

Despite feeling like you are stealing from Uncle Sam, you continue with the practice. Who's the master, God or money?

In both of these cases the fear of not having enough drove a decision not aligned with the values and principles we believe as Christians. The first lacked trust in God. The second was stealing.

If you feel a little uncomfortable right now, you are not alone. Many people have a desire to give more but the fear of lack drives their response. And so, instead of giving generously, we only give a small portion in order to save enough for ourselves. We are not being intentional about our giving. Therefore, we are not intentional in our living.

After Jesus talks to the people about giving he immediately follows up with "don't worry." I imagine that Jesus was sitting on the side of the mountain giving his sermon and saw the faces of the people. I bet they looked exactly like you do right now — wide eyes and a big gulp in your throat.

The good news is that Jesus immediately tells them that God will give them all that they need. *"That is why I tell you not to worry about everyday life — whether you have enough food and drink or enough clothes to wear. Isn't life more important than food, and your body more than clothing?"* In Matthew 6:25, Jesus goes on to say, *"These things dominate the thoughts of unbelievers, but your heavenly Father already knows all your needs."*

When we choose purpose as our way of life, we no longer have to worry about our basic provisions. God promises to take care of us. In fact, if we give generously God makes some pretty big promises to us.

Malachi 3:10-17 outlines God's rules of giving. Let's take a look at this passage. First, is that God asks us to tithe. Some may debate whether a tithe means of full ten percent.

"Tithe" in Hebrew is "hammaaser" which means a tenth part. So yes, tithing means giving a tenth by definition. If you give more or less than that then you are giving an offering either above or below the tithe. God tells us in verse 10 that if we tithe he promises to bless us.

    This blessing is not just dropping an armload full of money into our bank accounts. God does promise to open the windows of heaven and *"pour out a blessing so great you won't have enough room to take it in."* But, he also promises to protect what we already have and stretch it to the maximum. Verse 11 reads, *"Your crops will be abundant, for I will guard them from insects and disease. Your grapes will not fall from the vine before they are ripe..."* Maximum harvest! Our ideas, our businesses, our projects, our good works will be on the vine until they are so ripe that we get the maximum benefit from them. This is what God promises.

This is a law that God uses like gravity or acceleration. It's a system that cannot be broken because, *"Those who do evil get rich and those who dare God to punish them suffer no harm."* If you are a generous giver, it is God's nature to bless you so that you can give even more. This passage is so true that even sinners who follow this giving principle get rich. So then what's the point?

Glad you asked. Here's the difference in purposeful giving for God and just giving money for charitable reasons. The principle is found in Proverbs 15:6. *"There is treasure in the house of the godly, but the earnings of the wicked bring trouble."* Have you ever seen a person whom you thought had it all: fame, wealth and riches, yet they were miserable? The tabloids and gossip columns in the grocery store are full of tragic stories about people who achieved fame and riches, yet could never close the painful hole inside of them. Many turned to drugs and alcohol which ultimately consumed their lives to the last breath.

Riches and wealth are not a sign of godliness. Peace and joy with those riches are a sign of treasure produced by God. I'm not a prosperity gospel person. I don't believe everybody in Christ is going to be a millionaire. But I also don't believe that being a Christian means that you are broke and in debt. This passage in Malachi and other passages on wealth in the bible let me know this truth. We can have money; lots of it. We cannot put money ahead of God; none of it.

A big way we hinder the purpose in our lives is by being stingy — not giving generously to our churches, communities and people in need. When we do this we put our trust in money ahead of our trust in God. Purposeful living means trusting God in all areas of our lives. It means giving the best of what God has given us to do good work.

Giving is a form of evangelism — telling people about Jesus. When you feed the hungry and clothe the poor, God uses you to answer prayers. When a single mother prays for guidance with her son and you sign up to be a mentor for young boys, she knows God answered her prayer. When you pay your tithe to the church and the church in turn provides free summer meals for children who would normally eat free lunch in school, you draw those children and their parents closer to God. When you give, you shine God's light in the world. Give generously, on purpose.

BIBLE STUDY

Read Malachi 3:10-17. How does this passage relate to you in your current life? What things can God give you? What things will he protect in your life? What are you waiting on God to bless you with?

Reflecting on 2 Corinthians 9:7, how can you give more from what you have, rather than what you have left? Make a list of "stuff" that you can give to those in need. Now make a shopping list to buy a few new things for those in need, e.g., backpacks for school children, books for schools, toothbrushes and toiletries for homeless shelters, etc.

Journal Your Thoughts

8

Tell Somebody

What does it mean to be a disciple? The dictionary defines a disciple (of any kind) as one who accepts and lives the doctrine (opinions and teachings) of another. Therefore a disciple of Jesus Christ is one who accepts and lives his teaching. If you are a disciple of Jesus or if you are considering Christianity as a way of life, you have to know what that means.

For those of us who have already accepted Jesus as our Lord and Savior, we have a purpose to tell people about Jesus. Jesus was very clear in his words (read the red letters) around this.

Christians are often criticized for talking about their faith. Names like "bible thumper" and "holy roller" have emerged as a result of the proselytizing efforts of Christians. Though there may be diversity in our methods for sharing the faith, there can be no debate as to whether or not we, as Christians, should share the good news of Jesus. It was the last thing He said.

It's called the Great Commission.
Matthew 28:19-20

"Therefore, go and make disciples of all the nations, baptizing them in the name of the Father and the Son and the Holy Spirit. Teach these new disciples to obey all the commands I have given you. And be sure of this: I am with you always even to the end of the age."

When people ask me why I have to be so vocal about my faith, my answer is: "Because Jesus told me to." Sharing the faith is intrinsic to what we believe. The term we use when sharing our faith is "evangelism." It's a big and intimidating word and conjures thoughts of men on street corners shouting at you and hitting you in the face with tracts that warn of world destruction. So for the purposes of our discussion we are going to call "evangelism" what it is — telling people about Jesus.

Before we discuss what it is, let's talk about what "the big E" is not. It is not offending people of other religions. It is not telling your cousin he's going to hell if he doesn't get right. It is not telling the neighborhood bully God is going to strike him down. It is not in any way, shape, form or fashion — offensive or harmful to others.

Jesus is love. Jesus taught love. Jesus said that love is the greatest commandment. As Christians we tell other people about Christ because we love them. We love them so much that we want them to know what we know. God is good…all the time.

Every Christian is called to talk about Jesus in some way. God created you with this ability. Sure, some people have the gift of evangelism and they shout from the rooftops that Jesus is Lord. I use my books, blogs, videos, and teaching to tell people about Jesus. It's easy for me because I have the grace to do it and do it often. But, that does't let you off the hook.

You don't need to have the gift of evangelism to share the message. Some of you are introverts and will share only with family and close friends. You may not be comfortable sharing with words but you can still share the message. You may recommend this book to someone or suggest for them to watch a pastor on TV. Some of you extroverts will post on Instagram and groove at the family BBQ while talking about the water to wine miracle of Jesus.

You were created perfectly to do exactly what God has asked you to do. Tell others about Jesus. There will always be an opportunity for your to share your faith. You know why? Because Jesus told us to.

Let's handle some common objections to talking about Jesus. Let's start with "that's the pastor's job." Nope, the pastor's job is to teach us how to be better Christians. The pastor, as a vocation, is actually called to care for and encourage people who are already Christians. It is your job to go out and put into action what you have learned from your pastor. The bible says, *"... And if someone asks about your hope as a believer, always be ready to explain it. But do this in a gentle and respectful way."* (1 Peter 3:15-16) You should be ready to tell people why you believe in Jesus if someone asks. You may not be a proactive evangelist;

but you are responsible for giving an answer to those that ask about your faith.

You're shy and you don't know how to talk to people about faith. Maybe you feel like you don't know enough about the Bible to talk about your faith. No worries! The Holy Spirit has you covered. Matthew 10:20 says, *"For it is not you who will be speaking — it will be the Spirit of your father speaking through you."* So don't worry about what to say. When the time comes, God will put the words in your mouth.

Maybe you don't mind sharing your faith but you are too busy going about your day. You don't really think about it. Living on purpose should be our first priority. We should never be too busy for purposeful and meaningful dialogue with others about Jesus. Matthew 6:33 says, *"But seek first his kingdom and his righteousness, and all these things will be given to you as well."* When you're too busy dealing with real life issues remember that it is

God's job is to care for you. It's your job to worship, fellowship, evangelize, give and serve others.

You believe that your faith is private. It's just between you and God. Let me ask you this... if you were in a burning house and you saw a way out would you tell the rest of your family? Of course you would. Well, Christianity is a way out of the death and destruction of human life. It's a way to cope with the pain and trials of human existence. Jesus offers us eternal life. Don't you want your friends and family to experience that life? Jesus loves everyone and the Lord wants everyone to be saved.

Not unlike your relationship with your spouse or significant other, your relationship with Christ is intimate but it is not private. You have intimate moments that you don't share publicly, but people probably know that you are married, right? Some things about your faith will be between you and God, but letting people know you are the bride of Christ — married to Jesus — that's part of your purpose. Sharing the message of Jesus Christ is the best way to help change the lives of those you love.

These are just a few common excuses people use to keep the faith quiet. For each one there is a scripture to remind you that sharing your faith is a part of your purpose. When you find your purpose and start to live it, please share your experience with others to help them live more meaningful lives.

You need a personal strategy — an intentional and deliberate plan — to share you faith. Paul had a strategy. The Jewish people did not trust that Paul had been converted so he had a tough time sharing with them — understandably so. *"Every Sabbath he reasoned in the synagogue, trying to persuade the Jews and Greeks....Paul devoted himself exclusively to preaching, testifying to the Jews that Jesus was the Messiah. But when they opposed Paul and become abusive, he shook out his clothes in protest and said, 'Your blood be on your own heads! I am innocent of it. From now on I will go to the Gentiles.'"* (Acts 18:4-6)

Paul was not an effective messenger to the Jewish people. It wasn't his purpose. His life path, his personality, and his skill were more suited to telling non-Jewish people about Jesus. He was tremendously effective in that regard. You may not have the "gift" of evangelism to share your faith proactively, openly and aloud to everyone. However, you are perfectly suited to share your faith with the people whom God has chosen for you to share it.

Acts 4:1-22 shows us an example of evangelism at work. The disciples were doing what Jesus told them to do (v.2) before his ascension to heaven. They were fulfilling the Great Commission. Because they were working on purpose, the number of Christians grew daily. (v.4) This passage shows us that purposeful living fills us with Spirit and Power (v.8) and the disciples gave an answer for their power. (v.10)

It was evident to the people around them that they had walked with Jesus (v. 13) because they were not educated enough to know how to do the things they were doing. People could see what they had done (v.16) and it was their "doing" that produced faith in others.

It all comes down to this simple principle. When God is good, you have to tell it (v. 20) We can come up with many reasons for not sharing our faith. However, the bible gives us practical examples and specific instruction on how to tell others about Jesus. When you do what you were created to do, success is guaranteed. You were created to tell others about Jesus.

BIBLE STUDY

Read 1 Peter 3:15-17 aloud. How do you explain to people why you are a Christian?

In Acts 4:16, people saw what the disciples had done and they believed. What has God done in your life that you know it was only by his power that you could have done it?

What's your obstacle for not sharing the message of Jesus? How will you overcome it?

Do you believe in Jesus? If so, pray with me and read aloud:

Dear God, Thank you for sending your son, Jesus, to die for me. I know I am not perfect and I never will be. Please come into my heart. Direct my path so that I do what I am created to do for you. Forgive me of all my wrong-doing. Help me to forgive others. I don't know everything about the bible. I don't know a lot about how to be a Christian, but I now know and believe with my whole heart that Jesus is Lord. Amen.

If you prayed that prayer and you meant it, you are saved. You are a Christian and a member of the body of Christ. If you don't have a church where you worship regularly, I encourage you to visit churches and choose one to be your home. Tell the pastor Kamryn sent you.

Send us and email at shine@kamrynadams.com and let us know that you have decided to follow Jesus and his purpose for your life.

Journal Your Thoughts

PART II

THE GIFTS

Manifestation Gifts

- Knowledge
- Discernment
- Faith
- Healing
- Miracles
- Wisdom

Ministry Gifts

- Apostleship
- Prophecy
- Pastoring/Shepherding
- Evangelism
- Teaching

Talent Gifts

- Administration
- Craftsmanship
- Exhortation
- Giving
- Helps
- Hospitality
- Intercession
- Leadership
- Mercy
- Service

There are several websites where you can take gift asessments. Choose the one that best suits you. Each site has tools to help you better understand your spiritual gifts. The tool I use in the bible study class comes from:

www.giftstest.com

Take the assesment and identify your top five gifts.

THE GIFTS

We all have gifts that are intended for God's good work. Ephesians 2:10 says, "For we are God's masterpiece. He has created us anew in Christ Jesus, so we can do the good things he planned for us long ago." By gifts, we mean talents, skills, or abilities. We call them "gifts" because they were given to us by God when he created us. We didn't earn them so they were gifted to us.

We use our gifts to live our purpose to worship, fellowship, serve, give and tell others about Jesus. Our assignment from God is how we use our specific gifts, talents, and abilities to live out this purpose. We may have the same talents as someone else, but our personality and experience cause us to use the same gift in a different way.

For the purposes of this book we will focus on the spiritual gifts — the underlying ability that fuels our talent. For example, singers (talent) usually have the spiritual gift of exhortation. Painters (talent) have the gift of craftsmanship. We all have different talents that manifest from our spiritual gifts. "In his grace, God has given us different gifts for doing certain things well." (Romans 12:6)

When working together with different gifts you have to find your collective purpose as a group. Community and social organizations do this well. The organization will have a common goal and each member will bring their individual talent and skill to help achieve the goal. Every member plays a part to help fulfill the aims of the organization.

The body of Christ operates the same way. We all have different gifts to work together so that we shine God's light to those around us. Exodus 31 is an example of people with different gifts working together. When I read this passage, I immediately think of my experience in social and civic groups. Let's take a look.

Exodus 31 begins with God talking to Moses. He tells Moses that he has chosen a guy named Bezalel to help build the Ark of the Covenant. He says, *"I have filled him with the Spirit of God, giving him great wisdom, ability and expertise in all kinds of crafts."* (Exodus 31:3) God tells Moses that Bezalel is a *"master craftsman, expert in working with gold, silver, an bronze."* (Exodus 31:4) We see here that

Bezalel's gifts to work as a craftsman come from the Lord and God is using him to help Moses build the Ark of the Covenant - which was the wooden chest that held the ten commandments.

This very important task could be seen as common by some. Society tends to put a lower value or physical labor, but here we see God has great value in the craftsmanship of Bezalel. Craftsmanship is a spiritual gift given by God. It reflects his creative beauty in the world.

Not only did God choose Bezalel to be the master craftsman, but he appointed another guy, Oholiab, to be his assistant. He also called a team of other craftsman. Notice what God says to Moses in verse 6, *"Moreover, I have given special skill to all the gifted craftsmen so they can make all the things I have commanded you to make..."*

So, God told Bezalel, Oholiab and the craftsman to help Moses. However, he told

Moses specifically what to make. *"The craftsman must make everything as I have commanded you."* (Exodus 31:11) Moses, who had the gift of Leadership, was given the command, the vision of what to make. The others were there to build what God commanded Moses to do. God didn't tell all the craftsman the details of the project. He told Moses, the leader.

Though Moses was a great leader who had an intimate relationship with God. He was only able to complete his task by depending on the gifts of others. The craftsman, who had tremendous gifts from God, only knew what to do with those gifts through Moses' direction. They all needed each other to get the job done. No one person or no one gift is more important than another.

As you seek your purpose, you may get a clear answer with direction from God on what needs to be done. If you have gifts of leadership, administration, shepherding, service you may be given direct instructions from God. You'll hear a tiny voice in your heart, during prayer or Bible study that will tell you what to do. If you have gifts of craftsmanship, exhortation, giving or intercession, God will use your gifts to guide you into your purpose.

If you have the gift of giving, you may not hear a voice inside that says, "Give." However, if you have five dollars and someone needs to eat, God would very much like you to buy that person a sandwich.

If you have the gift of intercession (praying for others) and you know someone is having a hard time in life, you don't need them to ask you to pray. Just pray.

You don't need a burning bush to care for others. It's part of our purpose. When you worship, fellowship, serve, give, and tell people about Jesus, you do not require a separate word from the Lord. Yes! You are supposed to do it. Shine God's light in the lives of those around you. Without question, do good work.

There are three categories of spiritual gifts. We know this because there are three different words used in the original text when speaking of the gifts. In 1 Peter 4:10 the greek word, "charisma" is used. Charisma is translated at gift or talent. *"God has given each of you a gift from his great variety of spiritual gifts. Use them well to serve one another."* Yes, you have a gift. Everybody does. "Each of you" was given a gift from God for service to others. Examples of charisma gifts are leadership, service, hospitality, giving, administration, helps, mercy, and intercession.

In 1 Corinthians 12:7, Paul uses the word "phanerosis," which means manifestation. *"A spiritual gift is given to each of us so we can help each other."* These gifts are for the end recipient, not you. These particular gifts are experiences of God working through you for the benefit of another person. It is a manifestation of God in you. I call them the "gift card" gifts.

If I buy a gift card and mail it to my friend. The postman does not feel special because he got to deliver the gift card. He didn't stand at the doorway puffed up with pride when he handed her the gift card. When she opens the gift card she doesn't hug the postman. He's just the deliverer. When it comes to manifestation gifts, you are just the postman.

Healing is a manifestation (phanerosis) gift. It is not something that we possess like a talent (charisma) gift. When the Lord choses to manifest healing through one of his followers, he does so for the benefit of the sick. You may have the gift of healing. You may have laid your hands on someone or prayed over someone and they got instantly better. The next time someone was sick you tried to do the same thing and it didn't work. You know why? It's not you. It's God. Manifestation gifts are God flowing through you. So all my healers and prophets and tongue talking people, please don't get too caught up in the gift card. It's not for you. You are just the carrier.

The last category of gift can be found in Ephesians 4:11-13. *"Now these are the gifts Christ gave to the church..."* Neither charisma or phanerosis is used here. The word here for gift is "didomi" which is a verb to bestow or commit. These are gifts that God bestows upon some for the benefit of the church. They are listed in Ephesians. Apostleship, prophecy, evangelism, pastoring and teaching are all ministry (didomi) gifts. They are given with high responsibility to equip God's people to do good work.

So the three kinds of gifts are: talent gifts, manifestation gifts and ministry gifts. We possess talent gifts. Manifestation gifts are given when God works directly through us by the Holy Spirit. Ministry gifts are for those who are purposed to help the body of Christ grow and mature. We all have different gifts and we may have some gifts from each type. Learning to use these gifts for God's good work is our purpose. When we start living on purpose for God and using our gifts for good works, our lives are much fuller and we find the "more" we've been looking for.

Are these gifts only for Christians? Of course not. God created all people and we have free will to become Christians during our lives. Our gifts are assigned to us before we are born. God gives them to us for good works. However, not everybody uses their gifts for good.

Romans 11:29 tells us *"For God's gifts and his call can never be withdrawn."* You may be more familiar with the King James Version of this scripture that says, *"For the gifts and calling of God are without repentance."* This means that we have freedom to use our (charisma) gifts however we choose. God will not force us to do good works. You can take your gift of leadership and become a gang leader or you can become the founder of a non-profit. You can take your gift of administration and become a church trustee or you can become a drug lord. The choice is yours. One choice is purposeful and will bring joy and peace into your life. The other may bring riches but plenty of trouble with it - and likely some jail time.

It takes diligence and purposeful intention to use these gifts for God's good purpose. You have to make a decision that you want to live on purpose. You have to decide that the hole inside of you — the one that needs to be fed more and more — has got to heal. When you focus on being of service to others and doing good works, your life gets brighter because you are living in the center of God's light.

Remember, just because you have the same gift as your friend doesn't mean you have the same assignment. Your personality and life experience will dictate how you use those gifts. If you are an introvert with the gift of hospitality, your service will be very different from an extrovert with hospitality as a gift. If you are more people-focused, your gift of leadership will look differently than someone who is a more task-focused leader. This assignment is unique to you. You were a purpose before you were a person.

BIBLE STUDY

Read Romans 11:29 aloud. Think of some gifted people who are not using their talents for God's good work. How can you help them shift their mindset? What gifts might you have that are not being used for good works?

Read 1 Corinthians 12, the entire chapter. Write down what you have learned about the spiritual gifts. How can you work together with other gifted people for a common purpose?

Start thinking about how you can use your gifts in service to others.

Journal Your Thoughts

10

LIVING WITH GIFTS

Living with your gifts on purpose is a wonderful experience. You will shine God's light every day of your life. It will be marvelous, but it won't always be easy. It will be purposeful, but it won't always be pleasant.

Paul teaches us how to endure the hard times of purposeful living in 1 Corinthians 9:12. He says, *"We would rather put up with anything than be an obstacle to the Good News about Christ."* Purposeful living is a mindset that stays focused on showing the world that God loves us. Because we are on a mission, small nuisances and petty disagreements cannot disrupt our focus. In that same verse, Paul says that he gives up his rights so that the good works of God and the love of Jesus can be shared.

When we feel we have a right to something, our egos grow bigger and our hearts grow smaller. When you live on purpose, you waive your rights for good reason. You have a right to be treated nicely, but sometimes people are rude. Purposeful living means not retaliating against that rude behavior. You have a right to say whatever you want, but if those words are mean, purposeful living keeps you quiet. We give up our rights to shine our lights.

People are not the only obstacles to living on purpose. Being gifted can sometimes be an obstacle in itself. The gifts have potential blind spots that might cause you problems when working with others. You'll have to watch out for these blind spots.

Here are just a few....

People with the gifts of service, helps, and hospitality tend to be judgmental of those that don't have the gift. It is intuitive for you to serve when you see a need. You don't need to be asked to pitch in and help. When you see a person without the gift just sitting around, you may quickly judge that person as unhelpful or lazy. Instead of jumping to conclusions it will serve you well to simply ask for help. Some people need to be asked before they serve.

Those with discernment, prophecy and evangelism can be pushy and blunt. Your passion can turn into a forceful opinion that wounds others. We all need to tell people about Jesus but it is the Holy Spirit that will help them understand. Don't force it. Share your knowledge and don't take it personally when others don't agree with you. Remember to exercise the fruit the spirit. (Galatians 5:22)

People with teaching, wisdom and knowledge are easily sidetracked by new interests. The desire to learn new things is exciting but it takes focus and discipline to keep at it when newer, more exciting things come into your path. Use productivity tools and accountability partners to keep you on track.

Where are my exhorters? My faith people? And those who are gifted with intercessory prayer? You want people to feel better. You want to help solve problems and so you just might use the scripture out of context to prove your point. Those with this gift must be certain to speak God's word truthfully and allow God to bring about the good solution in His time. Don't force a happy ending to make people feel better.

Those with mercy and pastoring sometimes find themselves in hot water with the opposite gender. Their compassion is often misinterpreted as a more intimate desire than what was intended. Remember that broken people need your compassion and you have to be mindful that they are looking for love. Be caring and compassionate but set proper boundaries.

Givers and craftsman often want control of the things they do. They usually invest heart and soul into the task and because they fill a tangible need, it's easy to want to control where and how the your gift is used. Remember when we give of our time, talent or resources, it is for the use of another. Those with this gift must remember the definition of giving.

We can get so focused on our gifts that we neglect to remember the very reason we were given the gift — to do good works. 1 Timothy 4:16 reminds us to *"Keep a close watch on how you live and on your teaching."* Purposeful living requires active thought. You can no longer aimlessly move through life on auto pilot. Your responses to situations must be intentional. Your actions and behavior must be well thought out and deliberate. No more reactive living. Keep watch.

Fear is the most common obstacle in purposeful living. We are afraid of failure, of being ridiculed, or of being wrong. But you cannot let fear of failure keep you from using your gifts for God. Paul went boldly to Damascus to kill and imprison Christians. Jesus corrected his path. Go boldly in service with your gifts and let the Lord guide you.

In the Bible, 2 Timothy 1:7 lets us know that fear is not from God. Whenever you feel afraid, it is not God's purposeful intention for your life. *"For God has not given us a spirit of fear and timidity, but of power, love and self-discipline."*

Anger is another high hurdle on the path of purpose. Anger is a human emotion. Jesus got angry. The disciples got angry. People get angry. However, your response to anger must be willful. *"Human anger does not produce the righteousness God desires."* (James 1:20) A reactive, knee jerk response to anger will not produce good works. Paul warns the church at

Ephesus in Ephesians 4:26. *"And don't sin by letting anger control you."*

Anger can control the use of your gifts by making you resentful toward people whom you perceive are taking advantage of you. It can also be a reflection of your character that may discourage other people from hearing what you have to say.

Though fear and anger will hinder your walk, conformity is absolutely destructive to purposeful living. Trying to be like everyone else will annihilate your path and cause you to be lost in a wilderness of confusion. Paul teaches us about conformity. Romans 12:2 says, *"Do not copy the behavior and customs of this world, but let God transform you into a new person by changing the way you think. Then you will learn to know God's will for you, which is good and pleasing and perfect."*

I pray with all of my heart that after reading this book you will change the way you think. Every single time that I sit down to type on my computer while creating this project, I pray that God change the hearts and minds of every reader to draw them closer to him and clearer toward purpose. I declare that every assignment of every reader be completed to the perfection of Christ through the Holy Spirit. Let there not be one empty heart or clouded mind after reading this book. I pray this prayer each and every time in the name of Jesus, our Lord.

You will be a different person and that new person may not get along with the people you used to hang around. That new person may not like to watch the same things, listen to the same music or even eat the same foods. So you may not have a lot in common with your current friends. You will be more intentional about the way you live and for those who are not purpose partners — they may be left behind on the journey. This may include family and close friends. But don't turn back. Jesus said, *"No one who has left home or brothers or sisters or mother or father or children or fields for me and the gospel will fail to receive a hundred times as much in this present age; homes brothers, sisters, mothers, children and fields — along with persecutions and in the age to come eternal life."* (Mark 10:29-30)

Did you catch it? Living on purpose for God will provide a great return for your trouble in this life. Doing good for God doesn't get us to heaven. Grace does that. Doing for God provides blessings right here on earth — in this life. You will be blessed but there will be challenges along the way. The Lord will give you new friends, a new job, more people to love and people who love you, if you just follow Him. Don't conform.

Another reason many people don't live on purpose is that they feel unworthy of God's love or blessings. Poor-self image can keep you from accepting just how gifted you are. Maybe your parents never told you that you were talented or good at anything. Maybe people have made mean and disparaging remarks about you and you believe them. When you feel like you don't deserve God's blessings, remember that you were *"fearfully and wonderfully made."* (Psalm 139:14)

If nobody in the world sees your value — even if you don't — God knows how valuable you are to his plan. He needs you to dust yourself off, look in the mirror and say, "I have work to do."

Don't let poor self-image and low self-esteem keep you from living on purpose. There are counselors and coaches that can help build your esteem. Choose a Christian counselor who can help you understand how God sees you. Therapy can help you address the things in your past that keep you bound to low thinking. Somebody is out there waiting for you to use your gifts so they can see the light of God in the darkness of life. We need you.

Nobody wants to talk about the "s" word — sin. We try to dress it up and make it more comfortable to hear on Sunday mornings. Sin is anything in your life that is not godly. We all have sin in our lives.

We are saved by grace through Jesus Christ, but we do not continue to sin deliberately because of this grace. When we believe in the power of the Holy Ghost, things change in our lives. We don't do the things we used to do. Sin does not have a hold on our lives. We don't go around cussing folks out, gossiping, or being mean. We don't cheat on our spouses, abuse our children, or steal anymore. However, our lives will never be void of wrong-doing. We will never be perfect until Jesus comes. Don't chase perfection. Chase purpose.

The result of sin is death. Paul writes this in Romans 6:23. Later in Romans 7 he acknowledges the sin in his own life. Every day ask God for forgiveness for things you've done and things you may not even know you've done like hurting someone's feelings.

Many people think of sin as "big stuff" that other people do. But Jesus said that the greatest law is love and whenever we are not acting in love, we sin. Do you see any sin in your life? Look hard. 1 John 1:8 says, *"If we claim to be without sin, we deceive ourselves..."* You have sin in your life. Confess your sin to God and repent — say you're sorry and mean it.

Like anger, sin can shade our character and cause others not to see the light of Jesus in our lives. People won't listen to you when you tell them about God's love. Sin can also keep us stranded along the side of the purpose road. When you know you are not doing the right thing you tend to hide from people, from church, from purposeful living. Instead of going to God and asking forgiveness, we simply fade to the background. This is the wrong way to handle it.

Jesus said in John 6:39, *"And this is the will of God, that I should not lose even one of all those he has given me, but I that I should raise them up at the last day."* No matter what you have done, Jesus died for your sins. Don't be ashamed any longer. Ask God to forgive you and he will. Ask him every day.

Living with your gifts for God takes intentional and deliberate action. Don't be tossed around by people, pain or your past. Decide to live on purpose and ensure every thought, decision and action produces the good work of God.

BIBLE STUDY

Read and study Paul's passage in 1 Corinthians 9:12-18. What kinds of things might you have to put up with to serve others? What are some things you feel you have "rights" to that could hinder your service?

Read Romans 7:15 aloud. Now put this passage in your own words. What is it you keep doing that you wish you didn't? Ask God for forgiveness and be deliberate about not doing it anymore.

Now that you know your gifts, what are some obstacles or barriers that might hinder you? How will you over come them? Who can help you overcome them?

Journal Your Thoughts

11

Loving with Your Gifts

It is likely you have heard the 1 Corinthians 13 scripture on love. The reading usually starts at verse 4, "Love is patient; Love is kind." We read it at weddings. It's printed on t-shirts and key chains. We have embraced this passage as our "love" doctrine. Though we have taken this as a guide for our relationships, it is actually a service model.

Perhaps if we start at verse 1, we may have an easier time living verses 4-8. Verse 1 begins right after Paul teaches the church of Corinth about spiritual gifts. 1 Corinthians 13 isn't an isolated teaching on love. It is a continuation of Paul teaching how to use our spiritual gifts. In chapter 12, Paul teaches on spiritual gifts and reminds us we are together as one body in love.

He illustrates that the Body of Christ works like our human bodies — one body with many different parts that function differently. Each of the parts is equally important. Repeat it one more time aloud... each of the parts is equally important. No one gift is better than the other. No one type of service is more important than another.

It's the same with our human bodies. What's the most important part of your body? Some of you will say "heart" while others will say "brain." I'm pretty sure nobody said, "feet." However, who of you would like to have your feet cut off? You cannot walk without your feet. Your brain can signal all day long for you to walk across the room but you cannot do it without your feet. You need your feet and your brain.

Most people would agree that our hearts are more important than our heels, but we put lotion on our heels more consistently than we exercise our hearts. We wear shoes to keep from injuring our heels but we don't eat to prevent injury of our hearts. This is an important premise in the body of Christ. We must learn to care for the whole body. When one of our "parts" is missing or injured, we cannot move forward without them. *"If one part suffers, all the parts suffer with it, and if one part is honored all the parts are glad."* (1 Corinthians 12:26)

Love gives us the desire and the ability to care for the whole body. Love is not a feeling. It is a state of being. It's an action. It's a decision to live the way Jesus wants us to live.

Sometimes you'll feel like skipping down the road and handing out roses to everyone. Other days, love will be a decision to stay quiet instead of spouting out in anger.

Immediately after Paul teaches us how the body works together in Chapter 12, he goes on to say in Chapter 13:1, *"If I could speak all the languages of the earth and of angels but didn't love others, I would only be a noisy gong or a clanging cymbal. If I had the gift of prophecy, and if I understood all of God's secret plans and possessed all knowledge, and if I had such faith that I could move mountains but didn't love others I would be nothing."*

After talking to the Corinthians about using their gifts and encouraging them to work together, Paul tells them that love is the most important part of serving God and each other. You can read the pages of this book and flow in all of your gifts to the amazement of the world. You can serve, and give and read your bible three times a day. But, if you do not love others, none of it matters.

What does it mean to walk in love? In Romans 12:9 we're told *"Don't just pretend to love others. Really love them. Hate what is wrong. Hold tightly to what is good."* So we might not be blowing kisses and passing out flowers on the street corners, but living on purpose and in love means embracing what is good. God is good. So embrace God.

The rest of this passage through verse 18 goes on to give us specific instruction. It tells us to be genuine in our love and honor each other. It tells us never to be lazy and to work hard and serve the Lord with a good attitude. Love means being patient in trouble and helping others in need. It means we are prayerful and live in harmony with each other. When we put these behaviors into action in our lives, we have the fuel to run along more purposeful paths.

It is much easier to give, serve, lead or build when you are in harmony with others. How much more effective will you be as an exhorter or intercessor if you have a genuine love for the people around you? How much more contagious is our faith and powerful is our evangelism if we are patient in times of trouble? Yes, love is the fuel that allows us to get going on the road to purpose.

Whether great works of ministry or small acts of service, God is most glorified when we serve in love. Exhortation from the pulpit is just as important to God as exhortation in the coffee shop. Some people are called to ministry in church while others are called to serve in business, schools, government, and the global marketplace.

Wherever your purpose path leads you, remember Psalm 37:5. *"Commit everything you do to the Lord. Trust him and he will help you."*

BIBLE STUDY

When you think of "love" what comes to mind?

Read 1 Corinthians 12 and 13 together. How does this change your perspective on the "love poem" that we often hear at weddings? How would the material in 1 Corinthians 12 be helpful to newlyweds? Why do you think Paul had to write this letter to the Corinthian Church?

How is the illustration of love in 1 Corinthians 13:4-7 beneficial beyond our relationships in our service to others?

Journal Your Thoughts

12

LIFE PURPOSE STATEMENT

Purpose is the way in which we fulfill God's intention for our lives. It makes our living meaningful and our doing more effective. Your life purpose statement helps you remember who you are and why you were created. When the ups and downs of life start tossing you around on the purpose path, you will have this statement as your anchor.

A life purpose statement is two to four sentences that define who you are and why. As you create your life purpose statement, get feedback from others who partner with you on this journey. As you create the words, read them aloud over and over and see if they resonate with you.

Your life purpose statement is about who you are, so use "I AM" statements. Think about the gifts you have and your personality. Think about what comes easy for you and what you have a passion to do; for example, "I AM a skilled and helpful servant of God."

A very important part of knowing who you are is defining who you are NOT. This statement will help guide your decision making. Knowing who you aren't will eliminate guilt and uncertainty when making decisions e.g., "I AM NOT purposed to speak in front of a group. I work behind the scenes."

It's not enough to know who you are, but you must understand WHY you are. You were a purpose before you were a person. What need does God want to fill using your gifts, talents, personality and life experience. e.g., "I AM organized and focused to help complete the many tasks that are needed to make a project or event successful."

Lastly incorporate your passion into your purpose statement. Remember God gave you the desires in your heart. "I AM energized and excited when I help others relax and focus."

Using the examples above we just created the following life purpose statement:

"I am a skilled and helpful servant of God. I am not purposed to speak in front of a group, but I work diligently behind the scenes. I am organized and focused to help complete the many tasks that are needed to make a project or an event successful. I am energized and excited when I see others benefit from my behind the scenes work."

Based upon the life purpose statement above and using the definitions of the spiritual gifts, what gifts do you believe this person has? It should be very apparent that helps and hospitality are major gifts in the purpose life of this person. It looks like they may have administration, exhortation or possibly craftsmanship.

So, when the committee chair comes to this person and asks "Can you give the welcome address at the ushers retreat?" I'm sure the answer will be a confident and compassionate, "No." There may be other roles to play at the retreat but speaking in front of the group is not one of them.

When the boss asks if this person can run the project plan for an upcoming merger, the answer will likely be "yes." Not only can this person do the job but they will likely enjoy it a great deal.

The life purpose statement is about who you are. Be honest with yourself and be obedient to what the Lord has shown you. You may not want to accept your call to teach Sunday school, but if it's part of your "Nineveh" then start making a plan for it now, young Jonah.

I bind up fear and self-doubt and I loose the confidence of Christ into every reader so that you can complete this life purpose statement with a level of authenticity that you've never experienced before.

LETS GET STARTED...

Make a list of all the words that could be included in your purpose statement. Words that embrace your gifts, what others say about you, things you are really good at and things that make you happy and fulfilled. e.g., family, worship, wisdom, outside, easy-going, etc. First list them without giving it too much thought. Then, go back through the notes you've collected as you read this book. What jumps out at you?

After making your list of words, what themes do you see? What gifts did you think about our talk about most? What did you get excited about as you read through your notes? Is it leading, performing, executing, family, church, business? Write the theme and circle it.

Now use two to four sentences and write your Life Purpose statement using the theme and words related to that theme. Use the example above to help you.

Once you have your life purpose statement...and it may take you a few days...then move on to the next chapter and build your life purpose plan.

Craft your statement. Use the following to help you think about WHO and WHY you are.

I AM... (consider your gifts and personality)

I AM NOT... (consider your personality)

I AM... (your biggest gift) because.... (why do you think you were created?)

I AM EXCITED when... (consider your passion)

Write your LIFE PURPOSE STATEMENT:

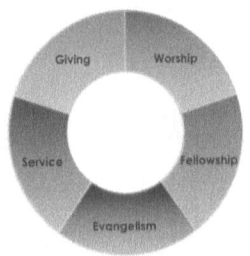

LIFE PURPOSE PLAN

You know who you are but its hard to remember who you are when the trials of life start to toss you around. So having a plan to go back to is helpful. The Life Purpose Plan will help you maintain clarity on what you are supposed to do. It will keep you focused on your assignment and keep you encouraged along the way.

Rate yourself in each of the areas of God's purpose for our lives.

1=not doing 2= just started 3=growing 4=consistently doing

WORSHIP: _____
FELLOWSHIP: _____
EVANGELISM: _____
SERVICE: _____
GIVING: _____

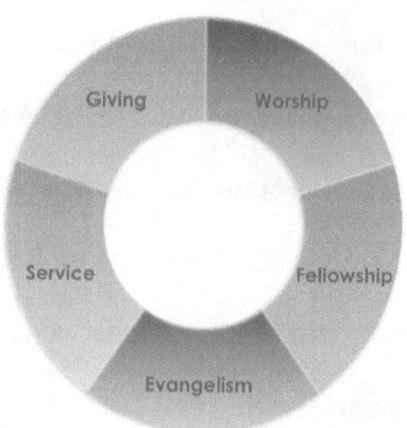

What is your best area on the life wheel?

_____

What is your least area on the life wheel?

_____

Use the journal notes you've collected over the course of reading this book to help you.

Why did you choose the above areas as "best" and "least"?

_____
_____
_____
_____
_____
_____
_____
_____
_____
_____

The goal is to leverage your strong areas and develop your weaker areas. You don't want to spend all your time focused on improving your weakness. You'll need to develop a level of self-acceptance about who you are. Celebrate your strength and maturity where you excel. Use your strong traits to serve God while developing your weaker traits of service.

For example, if your stronger area is fellowship and your weaker area is giving. Figure out how to incorporate a giving component into your fellowship time. Perhaps you pay for lunch or bring a gift for everyone when you meet. Maybe you can organize a philanthropic activity for you and your friends. Don't let this exercise overwhlem you. Be who you are for God while striving to be the best YOU that you can be.

Let's continue...

What are 3 things you can START doing to live on purpose for God? Be specific, e.g., exercise 3x a week, volunteer at a nursing home, etc.

Read your life purpose statment. Using your gifts and the passion you have, choose specific actions you will take to live on purpose. This can be something you do at church, home, work, school or the community.

#1 _____

#2 _____

#3 _____

What has kept you from starting these things before now? Think about it and be honest with yourself.

_____
_____
_____
_____

When will you start?

Give a specific deadline to begin each task.

Task #1 _____

Task #2 _____

Task #3 _____

What resources do you need to take action on your plan? i.e., raise money, make time, skill development, etc.

_____

_____

_____

What 2 things do you need to STOP doing in order to live on purpose for God? e.g., stop watching TV, doubting myself, gossiping, etc.

Reflect on those things that get in the way of you truly being who you were created to be. Be specific.

#1 _____

#2 _____

What obstacles are in the way of you living on purpose? These can be people, places or things. They can be external forces or internal struggles.

_____
_____
_____
_____
_____

How will you overcome these obstacles?

_____
_____
_____
_____
_____

Who can help you stay accountable to this plan? Do you need a counselor or coach?

_____

When you are "ON PURPOSE" what will life look like for you? i.e., How will you feel, think and act? Who will be around you?

_____
_____
_____
_____
_____
_____

How will you benefit from achieving your life purpose?

_____
_____
_____
_____
_____
_____

NOW LET'S BRING IT ALL TOGETHER!

How will I spend more time with God?

_____

_____

How will I fellowship with other Christians?

_____

_____

Who will I tell about Jesus? How will I do it?

_____

_____

_____

What will I do to serve others in church and community?

_____

_____

What will I do to give more? How much will I give?

_____

_____

IN CONCLUSION

Habakkuk 2:2 instructs us to write the vision and make it plain so that we can run with it. Writing your goals down on paper helps you remain accountable to what you want to to achieve. It helps you remember what is truly important in the toughest times of life. Use the last journal pages of this book to collect your thoughts on your new life.

If you took the time to write on the journal pages of this book, you are already poised for success. The act of grabbbing the pen or pencil and writing leaves an impression on your brain. You are focused! Reading this book has planted scripture in your heart. You are fed!

Your life is a journey towards God. There is no end to life in Christ. It is eternal life that after our days on earth will be spent in heaven. So don't chase purpose as destination. Chase it as a way of life. You are a human being. Never forget to "be" while you are doing.

Purposeful living is the "good life." It's not perfect and we will have our struggles, but the peace of God rests in our hearts. We get joy in the little things and celebrate every day as a victory. You have a plan. You know why you are here and what you are supposed to do. You are the only person for the job. You can't be fired, down-sized or replaced. It's you. God called you.

More from Kamryn Adams

Novels
Par for the Curse
When the Butterfly Falls
Gathering Moss

Non-Fiction
Stay in Your Lane

Blog
www.ShineTYC.com

Connect with Kamryn online
www.KamrynAdams.com
Facebook.com/thekamfam
Twitter.com/kamrynadams
Instagram.com/kamrynadams
Pintrest.com/kamrynpins
Youtube.com/kamrynadams

Journal Your Thoughts

www.ingramcontent.com/pod-product-compliance
Lightning Source LLC
Chambersburg PA
CBHW021126300426
44113CB00006B/304